A Primary Source Guide to

CANADA

Leslie C. Kaplan

The Rosen Publishing Group's

PowerKids Press™

PRIMARY SOURCE

New York

To Hadar

Published in 2005 by The Rosen Publishing Group, Inc.
29 East 21st Street, New York, NY 10010

First Edition
Editor: Rachel O'Connor
Book Design: Haley Wilson
Layout Design: Nick Sciacca
Photo Researcher: Adriana Skura

Photo Credits: Cover Image © John Lemker/Animals Animals; p. 4 © 2002 Geo Atlas, (inset) © Richard T. Nowitz/Corbis; p. 6 © Brian Miller/Animals Animals, (inset) © Ralph Reinhold/Animals Animals; p. 8 © Dagli Orti/Bibliotheque des Arts Decoratifs Paris/Art Archive, (inset) © Bettmann/Corbis; p. 10 © Will & Deni McIntyre/Photo Researchers, (inset) © Robert Copper/National Archives of Canada/PA-141503; p. 12 © Paul A. Soulders/Corbis, (inset) © Francis Lepine/Animals Animals; p. 14 © Erwin and Peggy Bauer/Animals Animals, (inset) © Megapress Images Inc; p. 16 © Nick Wheeler/Corbis; p. 18 © Queen's University at Kingston, Ontario, Canada/Bridgeman Art Library, (inset) Rufus F. Folkks/Corbis; p. 20 © Annie Griffiths/Corbis.

Library of Congress Cataloging-in-Publication Data

Kaplan, Leslie C.
A primary source guide to Canada / Leslie C. Kaplan.— 1st ed.
  p. cm. — (Countries of the world, a primary source journey)
Summary: Introduces the history, government, geography, and culture of Canada, along with other information about this vast North American nation.
Includes bibliographical references and index.
ISBN 1-4042-2750-4 (library binding)
1. Canada—Juvenile literature. [1. Canada.] I. Title. II. Series.
F1008.2 .K37 2005
971—dc22

                                    2003016526

Manufactured in the United States of America

Contents

A Big Country   5

Warmer in the South   7

The Making of a Country   9

Canada's Government   11

A Strong Economy   13

One Country, Many People   15

Holidays   17

Arts and Culture   19

Canada Today   21

Canada at a Glance   22

Glossary   23

Index   24

Primary Source List   24

Web Sites   24

Queen

Sverdrup Islands
Ellef
Ringnes
Island

King Christian I.

Loogheed I.

Bathurst
Island

Cornwallis
Island

Parry Channel

Banks
Island

Prince of Wales

Amundsen
Gulf

Prince Albert So.

Dolphin and Union Str.

**Victoria
Island**

McClintock Channel

Coronation
Gulf

Franklin Str.

Queen Maud
Gulf

King
William
Island

Somerset
Island

Gulf of Boothia

Committee B

Elizabeth

Islands

Jones Sound

Devon Island

Lancaster Sound

Bylot
Island

**Baffin
Bay**

Baffin Island

Davis Strait

Mackenzie
Bay

**YUKON
TERRITORY**

NORTHWEST TERRITORIES

CANADA

NUNAVUT TERRITORY

Southampton
Island

Prince
Charles
Island

**Foxe
Basin**

Hudson Strait

Coats
Island

Mansel
Island

Ungava
Bay

**Hudson
Bay**

BRITISH COLUMBIA

ALBERTA

SASKATCHEWAN

MANITOBA

Belcher
Islands

James
Bay

ONTARIO

NEWFOUNDLAND

QUÉBEC

Queen
Charlotte Is.

Vancouver
Island

PACIFIC
OCEAN

Québec

Montréal

OTTAWA

Toronto

Gulf of
St Lawrence

NEW
BRUNSWICK

NOVA SCOTIA

ATLANTIC
OCEAN

A Big Country

Canada is the second-largest country in the world. Only Russia is bigger. Canada has an area of about 3,800,000 square miles (9,841,955 sq km). It includes ten main areas called **provinces** and three territories. The territories are large areas of frozen land in the northernmost part of Canada, where very few people live.

Canada is a modern country with a **multicultural** society. Its total population is about 31,414,000. About three-quarters of all Canadians live in cities. Ottawa is the capital city. However, Toronto is the nation's most-populated city, with around 2,481,494 people.

◀ Canada lies between the Atlantic and Pacific oceans. To its south is the United States. *Inset:* Pictured here is a view of Toronto as seen across Lake Ontario. To the left is Toronto's famous CN Tower, which is 1,815 feet (553 m) tall.

5

Warmer in the South

Canada has four seasons. Winters can be very cold in much of the country. In January, **temperatures** drop to -4°F (-20°C) in many parts. In Canada's northernmost area, called the Arctic, temperatures stay below freezing almost all year. Most Canadians live along the southern border, which is the warmest part of Canada. There, temperatures in the summer are around 72°F (22°C), although the area gets snow in the winter just as the rest of the country does. Snowfalls in the Great Plains can last from late November through mid-March. The plains are flat areas where farmers grow grain. The plains occupy the provinces of Manitoba, Saskatchewan, and Alberta.

◀ Western Canada is known for its Rocky Mountains. Pictured here is Mount Robson in the Rockies, surrounded by clouds. *Inset:* Eastern Canada is home to the famous Niagara Falls. The falls are located in Ontario.

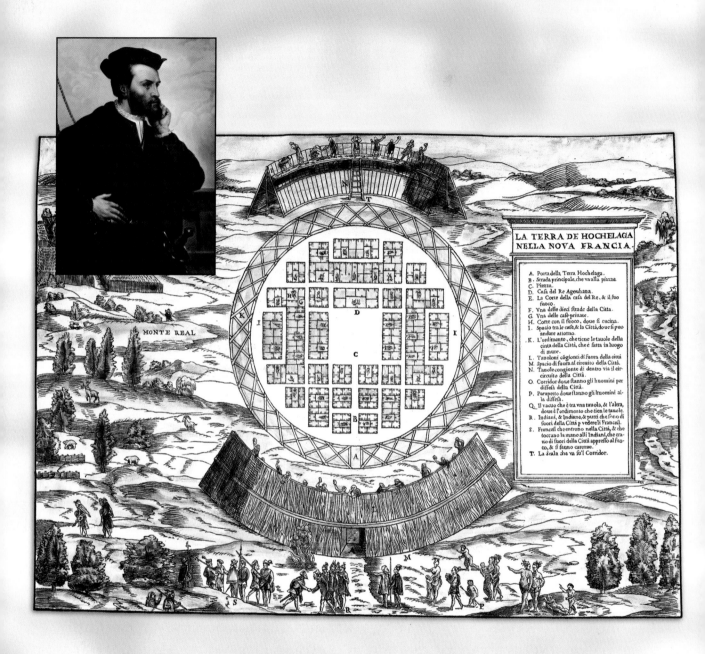

LA TERRA DE HOCHELAGA
NELLA NOVA FRANCIA.

A. Porta della Terra Hochelaga.
B. Strada principale, che va alla piazza.
C. Piazza.
D. Casa del Re Agouhanna.
E. La Corte della casa del Re, & il suo fuoco.
F. Vna delle dieci strade della Città.
G. Vna delle case priuate.
H. Come con il fuoco, doue si cucina.
I. Spacio tra le case, & la Città, doue si puo andare attorno.
K. L'ordimento, che tiene le tauole della cinta della Città, che è fatta in luogo di mure.
L. Tauoloni congionti di fuora della città
M. Spacio fuora al circuito della Città.
N. Tauole congionte di dentro via il circuito della Città.
O. Corridor doue stanno gli huomini per diffesa della Città.
P. Parapetto doue stanno gli huomini alla diffesa.
Q. Il vacuo che è tra vna tauola, & l'altra, doue è l'ordimento che tien le tauole.
R. Indiani, & Indiane, & putti che sono di fuori della Città p vedere li Francesi.
S. Francesi che entrono nella Città, & che toccano la mano alli Indiani, che erano di fuori della Città appresso al fuoco, & si fanno carezze.
T. La scala che va su'l Corridor.

MONTE REAL

8

The Making of a Country

Canada's first settlers, the Inuit, came from Siberia about 35,000 years ago. The Inuit are the **ancestors** of Canada's native Indians. In the 1400s, Europeans searching for a new sea route to the markets of Asia reached Canada. A strong fur trade with the Indians drew many French and British in the 1600s. Between 1689 and 1763 the French and the British fought each other for control of the land in Canada and elsewhere. Britain beat France in 1760, after fighting what is called the Seven Years' War. In 1867, Britain passed the British North America Act, which established Canada as a self-governing nation.

This map of Hochelaga, or today's Montréal, shows an Iroquois Indian settlement in the 1500s. *Inset:* Jacques Cartier was a French explorer who claimed areas of Canada for France, including Montréal. He gave Canada its name after hearing some Indians call their village *"Kanata." Kanata* means "village" in Iroquois.

Canada's Government

In the past, Britain's kings and queens ruled Canada. Today the queen of Britain is the **symbolic** leader of Canada. She has no real power to govern. The person who is at the head of the Canadian government is the prime minister. The prime minister does not get voted into office the way that an American president does. Rather, the Canadian prime minister is the leader of whichever political party gets the most members elected to a lawmaking body called Parliament. This is because Canada's form of government is a parliamentary **democracy**. Under this system, the prime minister and his cabinet must answer to the Parliament, which holds the power.

Shown here are the Parliament buildings in Ottawa. *Inset:* Queen Elizabeth II and the Canadian prime minister, Pierre Trudeau, signed the Canadian constitution in April 1982. The constitution gave Canada full independence from Britain.

A Strong Economy

Canada has a strong economy. In fact, in 2002, Canada underwent more economic growth than any other country in the world. Natural **resources** help to fuel Canada's **industries**. Paper and wood products are Canada's top **exports**. Farming is an important industry, and wheat is the major crop. **Tourism** creates a lot of business for Canada. Canada also makes much money from the sale of manufactured goods, such as cars, food, and computer software. Canadians have created many computer products and services that let people connect across great distances. This has helped Canada to become a leader in the **telecommunications** industry.

Canada is rich in natural resources, which include forests, lakes, fish, oil, and copper. This picture shows the inside of a copper mill in British Columbia. *Inset:* Shown here is a paper mill in Quebec. Paper is made from wood.

One Country, Many People

Canada is often called a **mosaic**, because it is home to many different **cultures**. Canadians come from every part of the world, and they often keep the ways and languages of their old countries. There are Canadian cities with strong Greek, Italian, and Chinese communities. Quebec City and Montréal are centers of French Canadian culture. People of French and British **descent** make up the two largest groups.

Canadians are known for their love of sports, especially ice hockey. This game was invented in Canada, and many of today's best hockey players are Canadian. Many Canadians love the outdoors. They like to go hiking and camping in the **wilderness**.

◀ Waterton Lakes National Park is one of Canada's many parks and wilderness areas where people like to hike. *Inset:* Shoppers walk along the streets of the French Canadian city of Montréal.

15

Holidays

The Canadian calendar is filled with holidays. Easter and Christmas are two of the most important religious days for Christian Canadians, who make up about 90 percent of the population. Canada Day is the most important national holiday. It takes place on July 1, the date that Canada gained independence from Britain in 1867. Canadians honor their country's birthday with fireworks and parades. Every year Quebec has a festival, or event, called Winter Carnival. In the summer, Toronto celebrates all its different cultures with a nine-day festival called the International Caravan. Other important Canadian holidays are New Year's Day on January 1, Labour Day, and Thanksgiving.

◄ In early February, Canada's Winter Carnival draws people from all around the world to Quebec. Shown here is the snow palace, a huge building made entirely from snow! Every year a castle is built especially for the carnival.

Arts and Culture

Canadian art began with the Inuit. As early as 600 B.C., Canada's first settlers made carvings from wood, ivory, and stone. In the 1920s, Canadian artists known as the Group of Seven became famous for painting colorful pictures of the Canadian wilderness. In 1957, Canada's government formed a special council to advance arts and culture. As a result, the country's museums, orchestras, and theaters have multiplied. After New York and Los Angeles, Toronto is North America's top film and TV **production** center. Toronto has also gained recognition for its modern **architecture**. The city's CN Tower is the world's tallest tower.

◀ This is a painting by one of the Group of Seven, Arthur Lismer. It is called *Quebec Village, 1926. Inset:* Pictured is Canadian actor Michael J. Fox.

Canada Today

Canadians live in a country that is respected throughout the world. Canadians are known as a friendly people and have a history of behaving peacefully with other nations. Canada joined the United Nations (UN), an international peacekeeping group, in 1945. Since then Canada has played an important role in UN efforts to solve problems between other countries. For such efforts, Canada is thought of as a good neighbor to the world. Canada is also considered to be one of the best countries in which to live. Its population enjoys a high rate of employment, good healthcare, and a strong educational system. Canada offers its people an excellent quality of life.

◀ Canada has a high standard of education. Ninety-seven percent of Canadians can read and write. This is a high percentage. Pictured here are schoolboys outside their school in Vancouver, British Columbia.

Canada at a Glance

Population: About 31,414,000

Capital City: Ottawa, population about 1,010,500

Largest City: Toronto, population about 2,481,494

Official Name: Dominion of Canada

National Anthem: "O Canada"

Land Area: 3,800,000 square miles (9,841,955 sq km)

Government: Parliamentary democracy

Unit of Money: Canadian dollar

Flag: Canada's flag has two red stripes on either side of a red maple leaf on a white background. The colors of red and white stand for strength and purity and are connected with Britain and France. The maple leaf is a symbol of Canada's many maple trees.

Glossary

ancestors (AN-ses-terz) Relatives who lived long ago.

architecture (AR-kih-tek-cher) The art of creating and making buildings.

cultures (KUL-churz) Beliefs, practices, and arts of different groups of people.

democracy (dih-MAH-kruh-see) A government that is run by the people.

descent (dih-SENT) The line of family from which someone comes.

exports (EK-sports) Goods sold by one country to another.

industries (IN-dus-treez) Moneymaking businesses in which many people work and make money producing a particular product.

mosaic (moh-ZAY-ik) A picture made by fitting together small pieces of stone, glass, or tile and cementing them in place.

multicultural (mul-tee-KULCH-rul) Composed of different groups of people.

production (pruh-DUK-shun) The method of making things.

provinces (PRAH-vins-ez) Main parts of a country.

resources (REE-sors-ez) Things that occur in nature and that can be used or sold, such as gold, coal, or wool.

symbolic (sim-BAH-lik) Relating to an object or a picture standing for something else.

telecommunications (teh-leh-kuh-myoo-nih-KAY-shunz) The science and technology of communication at a distance through use of such instruments as telephone, radio, or television.

temperatures (TEM-pruh-cherz) How hot or cold things are.

tourism (TUR-ih-zem) A business dealing with people who travel for fun.

wilderness (WIL-dur-nis) An area that has no lasting settlements.

Index

A
Alberta, 7
Arctic, 7

B
British North America Act, 9

C
Canada Day, 17
CN Tower, 19

E
economy, 13

exports, 13

G
Great Plains, 7
Group of Seven, 19

I
ice hockey, 15
International Caravan, 17
Inuit, 9, 19

M
Manitoba, 7
Montréal, 15

O
Ottawa, 5

P
Parliament, 11
prime minister, 11
provinces, 5, 7, 11

Q
Quebec City, 15, 17

S
Saskatchewan, 7
Seven Years' War, 9

T
telecommunications, 13
territories, 5, 11
Toronto, 5, 17, 19
tourism, 13

U
United Nations, 21

W
Winter Carnival, 17

Primary Source List

Cover. The Canadian Rockies. Photograph by John Lemker.

Page 4 (inset). The skyline of Toronto at night, seen across Lake Ontario. Photograph by Richard T. Nowitz, August 1992.

Page 8. This map of Hochelaga (present-day Montréal) was the first printed map of a settlement in North America. It was published in Venice, Italy, between 1556 and 1606.

Page 8 (inset). Portrait of Jacques Cartier. Painting by Theophile Hamel, circa 1844.

Page 10 (inset). Queen Elizabeth II and Canadian prime minister Pierre Trudeau photographed during the signing of the Constitution of 1982 on April 17, 1982.

Page 12. An interior view of the processing mill at Highland Valley Copper Mine in British Columbia, August 1994.

Page 16. Snow palace at Quebec City Winter Carnival. Photograph by Nik Wheeler, circa 1990.

Page 18. *Quebec Village, 1926*. By Arthur Lismer.

Page 18 (inset). Michael J. Fox. Photograph by Rufus F. Folkks, circa 2002.

Page 20. Uniformed Canadian and Chinese Canadian schoolboys outside their school in Vancouver, British Columbia. Photograph by Annie Griffiths Belt, March 1991.

Web Sites

Due to the changing nature of Internet links, PowerKids Press has developed an online list of Web sites related to the subject of this book. This site is updated regularly. Please use this link to access the list: www.powerkidslinks.com/cwpsj/pscana/

9106,4